Library of Emotions

Poems

of Lament and Hope

during the COVID-19 Pandemic

Patricia Campbell Kowal

ISBN: 978-1-64921-689-2

Printed in USA

Dedicated

to

Hope for the World

Contents

"We have a chance to do something extraordinary. As we head out of this pandemic, we can change the world. Create a world of love. A world where we are kind to each other. A world where we are kind no matter what class, race, what religion or lack of, or what job we have. Let love and kindness be our roadmap."

~Johnny Corn, American actor

From the author

I live in Washington State where the first confirmed COVID-19 case and cluster appeared in the United States. With family who reside in that initial epicenter, I wondered what may happen to my children, the country, the world, to me. Living in a virus-induced pandemic atop a globally endangered environment, an underlying racial divide and volatile rhetoric from leaders in power, life felt unnerving at best.

From mid-March to early June 2020, writing helped me contemplate losses and possibilities born of the coronavirus pandemic, coupled with the impactful civil rights demonstrations in over 600 U.S. cities and abroad. As I wrote, poetry emerged and became good medicine for my soul. A theme appeared as the poems accumulated. I noticed a refrain of lament and hope. Along with the world on edge, I observed vivid examples of fear and love, hate and grace, indifference and engagement, and death and life, punctuating daily existence in this extraordinary time.

I offer these poems to ponder in this period of great challenge with an invitation to peer into your personal library of emotions—your heart.

May I suggest as you peruse this chapbook, perhaps read just one or two poems a day, then ask, *What word or phrase resonates with me and to what does it call me?* May your answers bless you, and may you find hope in the lament we face together.

Coronavirus Disease of 2019

COVID-19
The acronym
Like military jargon
Alphabet soup easier to speak
Harder to banish
Contagious as fear
Superbug
Invisible to the naked eye
Superman's match
Spreads in leaps and bounds
Slips onto prey with a single handshake
Lurks on elevator buttons, doorknobs, boxes
Moves worldwide on ships, planes, trains
Lethal in nursing homes
Seizes the most vulnerable
Prolific in public
Grabs unsuspecting strong
Travels on happenstance
Silent, deadly
Stuns a world that seeks refuge from the storm

COVID-19, you took one of my own, Easter Sunday,
of all days
Not on purpose, I suppose
I wonder what kind of messenger you are

Solitude or Loneliness

Pandemic
World threat to wellness
Reduce the curve
Curb your contacts
Mitigate
Stay six feet away
Wear a mask
Wash your hands
with soap and water
for twenty seconds
(singing Happy Birthday twice)
Best not travel on public transit
Stay at home

Perhaps this is the time to
be the best you can be
Communicate frequently with loved ones
Reinvent activities
Play outside, safely
Read
Clear space
Reach out, be open to receive
Hunker down
Pray
In your retreat, think about this—

The difference between solitude and loneliness
is whether or not I like the person I'm with

Then love yourself, others, the world

Spring

You wore your poem
        when rain fell lightly
        and dark nights shortened
You wore your poem
        when you arrived
        and frosted land softened
You wore your poem
        when bulbs unfurled
        and daffodils blossomed
You wore your poem
        when trees dropped blooms
        and green leaves sprouted

Indeed,

You wore your poem
        when medics cared
        and offered patients comfort
You wore your poem
        when people honored elders
        and visited from a distance
You wore your poem
        when musicians rendered song
        and the world swayed in cadence
You wore your poem
        when people demonstrated en masse
        and birthed a new civil rights movement

Spring, your wardrobe, your presence
        wrapped us in apt awareness
        and promised buds of hope

Holy Instant

The world trembles
Inhabitants scramble in uncertainty
How to meet each moment?
What is fundamental to be safe?

Perhaps like the ocean
    when the surface is raging
    there is calm below

Can one find a stillness?
Can one breathe in peace in the throes of trouble?
Can one hold space with love for all?

Rest in the Holy Instant of truth, Love
One moment at a time

Healing Light

Full moon shines at night
Fireball sun peeps at dawn
Pandemic rages

People seek healing
Bright glow from the sky beckons
Souls that cry for light

Greatest Hope of All

If I speak in tongues of people and angels, but have no
hope
I am only a resounding menace or a clanging noise
If I live through tumult and offer no hope
I am only a self-centered clod

Hope is curious, hope is bold
It does not disappoint, it is not angry
It is not critical, it is not defensive
It is not easily cast aside, it keeps no record of injury
Hope does not delight in disappointment
But rejoices in healing
It always holds one up, always embraces,
Always wants the best, is always available
Hope never intends hurt

Though faith, hope and love are gifts
The greatest hope of all is
Faith and love will persist

Library of Emotions

So many books on the shelves
Like pan-faced soldiers in formation
Lined up in library stacks
Spines with myriad colors, titles describing contents
Pick the yellow-bound trade back, *Happy*
Turn its pages to find joy, peace, calm
Or the hard-covered blue one, *Depressed*
Inside chapters, dark, sad, recessed
The thick green tome, *Envy*
Jealousies between the covers
Oh, the red one, *Anger*
Even the pages feel hot as you thumb through them

Volumes remain
Digests entitled *Surreal, Tired, Curious, Confused,*
Exhausted, Cooped Up, Relieved
Stop. Think. Reframe.

Which emotions are alive in you?
Give each feeling a name
Acknowledge their presence
Hold them, sit with them on your lap
Take care of them
Like you would any good book that speaks to the
heart

The Great Pause

The world at a standstill
Like a still frame in a movie
Where we are the characters in the picture
Some too busy, others too angry
Maybe over-spending, under-loving, in distress
Perhaps a Pollyanna or an ignoramus
Unable to weed the urgent from the important

Think outside the box
Instead of COVID-19 pandemic
Consider it the Great Pause
Like the gift of sabbatical
Time
  for introspection, for gratitude
  to be, to grieve
  to write, to walk
  to exercise your passion

When the Great Pause ends, beware!
Televisions will bombard you with buy this or that
Magazines will scream be sheik
Politicians more interested in a vote will minimize the
  damage
Organizations will call you; will you overcommit?

May the Great Pause show mercy
Perhaps a once in a lifetime gift
A lesson of grace on how to practice small pauses
  each day

Betwixt and Between

pandemic
    liminal space
    betwixt and between
    not this, not that

like
    shipwrecks awaiting rescue
    nations recovering from war
    prisoners contemplating release

uncertainty
    something different looms
    life no longer the same
    choice is of essence

practice
    surrender
    caring and sharing
    new consciousness

pandemic
    liminal space
    betwixt and between
    perhaps this, perhaps that

Empty Vessels

The people shout, demand
Guns slung over their shoulders at capital buildings
Swastikas on their sleeves
"The empty vessels make the loudest noise,"
    Shakespeare wrote
Hateful minds breed hateful hearts

Choose peace for yourself
Let a still, small voice be the guidance
Touch with love, be kind, be just
Remember Martin Luther King's cry, *I Have a Dream*
March with your vulnerable heart on your sleeve
    instead

Dying into Life

I am dying
    I am living
I shelter in place
    I have freed-up time
I distance
    I find myself
He died
    I am alive

So, dear one
    what are you called to as viral, racist, and
    environmental pandemics surround you
    as you are dying into life?

What to Embrace?

Pandemic rages
much uncertainty
World in pain
victims abound
Some well
others not
Peoples' plans squelched
stay-at-home
Social distancing
new normal
Public servants
at risk
Extra friendly
folks reach out
Vision with love
care offered
Song rings from Italian balconies
connects the world
Applause resounds in New York City
caregivers honored

Through the door of pandemic
what is seen?
With change in the world
what is felt?
What needs one's embrace?
who needs an embrace?

Equanimity

I once worked with someone
Who exuded even-mindedness
I overheard another speak,
"How does she always stay calm in life's
    challenges?"
Chaos all around, but she
Steady as a rock
Empathetic as a caring teacher

Equanimity
The ground for wisdom and freedom
The protector of compassion and love

I think of Jesus's mother, Mary
Nelson Mandela, the Dalai Lama,
Miss Banks, my piano teacher
Thich Nhat Hanh, Marianne Williamson
My co-worker
All ambassadors of the cosmos
In their lifetimes have they
  Woken up and smiled before they stepped out of
    bed?
  Mindfully eaten breakfast with gratitude?
  Sweat once a day while they moved their bodies?
  Chosen enlightened reading, been quiet, sat,
    napped, walked meditatively?
  Reached out to loved ones and others?

What would it be like if each of us practiced
  equanimity in difficult times, or anytime at all?

Strangest of Times

The strangest of times
        and its lessons
The chaos of a dream
        and the grandeur
The craziness of nature
        and her beauty
The absurdity of stupidity
        and its innocence
The notion of forgiveness
        and its healing
The pain of birth
        and its gift
The frustration of silence
        and its wisdom
The thorns of roses
        and their blossoms
The grief in loss
        and its completeness
The mystery of reality
        and its truth
The broken from brutality
        and new awareness
The practice of perfectionism
        and its impossibility
The angst of unknowing
        and its protection
The curse of pandemic
        and its blessing

No Order, Only Sequence

No order, only sequence
COVID-19 →world encircled
Infection→ sickness
Wash hands→ dry skin
Stock up on toilet paper→ what the heck
Social distancing→ virtual hugs
Gym closed→ walk instead
No work→no paycheck
Food scarce→find food banks
Only sequence, no order

Bliss Ninny

Bliss ninny
Over-the-top
Can't you meet me
Where I'm at?

I'm so sad
You act too happy
Please be sensitive
Not slappy, clappy

Overdramatic, overdone
Know a quiet mind will better do
To calm the hurt inside
To help the pain move through

Earth Shudders

Earth shudders
Shivers from fever of the moment
Convulses in agony, nothing is the same
Virus runs rampant
People succumb, overwhelmed and breathless

What if the contagion could speak?
Like Pali
The Hawaiian goddess of fire and destruction
The voice shouts, "Beware! See me, hear me,
 rebalance!"

People scurry, declare war on the illness
Close borders, contain communities
Care for the sick and dying
Grieve their dead
Applaud their caregivers
Stop sickening the planet

Earth shows hope
Skies blue in China
Canals clear in Italy
Pollution eases in New York
Greenhouse effects lift
Nations help nations

Though everything appears unfamiliar
One message persists—
The call again, always
Join in compassion for others
Take care of our planetary home

This Day in April 2020

This day in April 2020 I saw
A supermoon
A super mom
The man in the moon
A man in a room
Horrific reports
Appalling retorts
The sun in the sky
A grandmother cry
Easter cards written
Dyed eggs broken
Statistics on COVID
Overwhelm of a medic
This day in April 2020 I saw
Wonders, distress
Hope more or less
The tension of opposites
Pulling, pushing
The role of fate
Fulfilling, crushing

Reset Button

Rebels are not much for rules
Perhaps they think they are for fools
Rebels often pay the price
Having to do things more than twice
In uncertain times it is hard to know
What outcomes will occur
If rebels could be open to learn
The reset button is their gift to discern

Breathe

The black man cannot breathe
Policeman, knee to victim's neck
"Please, I can't breathe"
Last words before he is dead

"Please, I can't breathe"
The brown man's call from the hospital bed
The medic there to save his life
Too late, could not keep him from the plight

Cold blooded murder amid pandemic
Patient's COVID death in midst of protest
A country shuttered for months
Pent up emotions explode in streets
Soldierly police on the beat

Pandemic of environmental pollution
Little agreement on solution
Endangered water and air quality
The poor, of color, suffer largely

Pandemic virus
Pandemic racism (a sin, the pope says)
Pandemic pollution
A global cry, "I can't breathe"

So many layers that strike to the core
Where deep fears already live
Could this collective trauma
Birth new breath into a broken world
With hope to find the dream

Of social justice and well-being
With no longer the cry, "I can't breathe?"

History instructs, Pandemic of 1918
World War I Armistice signed
Thousands exhale a sigh of relief, rally to celebrate
Inhale more contagion
A second wave, more harsh realities
Six times more than the war's fatalities

Pandemic of COVID-19
Hundreds of thousands succumb, more to come
While protests erupt against police brutality and the
  killing of the black man who could not breathe
Civil unrest explodes, distancing ignored
More deaths from the virus onboard
Voices cry out "We can't breathe"

What might it be
  If we all take a knee
    rather, to the ground
  And, with a bowed head
  Inhale forgiveness, love, social responsibility
  Exhale hatred, judgement, irresponsibility
  Pray for guidance to humbly see?
And hope
    our children's children can
    Breathe

Lament 2020

Uncertain times engulf the globe
Like a tight belt cinched one notch at a time
Cutting off ability to breathe

From a fixed hold around the earth's equator
Pain, fear, loneliness, exhaustion
rivets humanity to a worldly still point
Where death threatens vibrant lives, from illness to brutality

The feeling you wonder?
What is this apocalyptic sense that changed the world in only weeks, months?
I say the word aloud, LAMENT
Lament. Deep sadness. Wailing of the heart.

Look inside, find your sadness
Until we deal with our grief, we cannot move forward
Give lament its voice
Cry from the soul and connect with the wisdom of our oneness with all

Natural State

Natural state
Present moment
Free, fluid
Agile, open
Peaceful, spacious
Receptive, responsive
Fearless, perceptive
Accesses care and wisdom
No matter what is going on
Inside or out

Let go the need of an addicted mind
Let go of bias
Let go of irrational fear
Practice sitting in your natural state
Hold your Inner Child close to you
Open your heart center
Absorb the energy
Let its vibration flow into daily life
Let it empower you
Your innocent natural state

Scaffolding

scaffolding, life-giving structure
underpinnings that change over time
like networks of wooden planks
supporting construction at higher levels
inviting entrance to the Upper Room

Full Speed to Full Stop 2020

Restaurant thriving one week
Closed the next
Dress shop, family owned, prospering
Shuttered

Hair salon, busy
Then empty
Sign on door, see you when we can

Airline, thriving
Suddenly, bankrupt
High school prom, cancelled
Traditional graduation, altered

Medical emergency
Stroke, heart attack, premature labor
Either survive with risk, or die
With no gathering to bury you

Vibrant this week
On a deathbed the next
It happens so fast
Full speed to full stop

The sense of whiplash
Life-long wounds, poverty for some
Crazy making for others

From a shutdown country, to mitigated re-
openings, to demonstrations in streets

Jerked and plummeted on the roller coaster of
ups and downs
Like a head-on crash, from full speed to full stop
Only to wake up, stunned, and you say, *What happened?*

Integration

A fundamental need
The sense of belonging
Every soul
A longing

Living the *either/or* way of life
Invites deep, relentless strife
Another way, *both/and,* inclusive thinking
Allows for integrated reckoning

Not sameness, but
Connection amid difference
No need to compromise sense of self
Simply, love your brother for world heart-health

No room for hate, oppression
Let fear abate
The call to action
Collective compassion

Compartmentalize none
Be open to all
Let others be your teachers
Live big, not small

More than Weather

Giddy
like when snowflakes tickle the nose
only weather

Content
like when a breeze whooshes through trees
only weather

Sad
like when dark clouds cover the sky
only weather

Blustery
like when windstorms strew branches
only weather

Cataclysmic
like when a tsunami washes over the world
earth shattering

In Times of Uncertainty

Times of uncertainty
Always around us
Yet sometimes, seemingly, more than others
  wartime, famine, raging fires, deluge, tornado,
  cancer, social injustice, brutality, civic unrest,
  pandemic, loss of loved ones, bodily injury, can't
  pay the bills, child is ill, mind is twisted,
  separation, you name it

Uncertainty lurks
The not knowing how or when
Fear, too near; love, too far

In times of uncertainty
Watch what animals do
Study the mystics
Listen closely
Share a voice
Cry easily, laugh regularly
Grieve losses
Write a letter
Ask for help
Sing, dance, play
Pray for guidance
Let the answers find you

In times of uncertainty, remember
Where we live is in the mind
Who we are is in the heart

Hits Home

The lump in the throat, like a burning coal
The churn in the gut, like milk curdling
My vulnerable cousin
A life taken by COVID-19
Fifty years old
At risk, paralyzed from the neck down
Wheelchair bound for thirty-five years
Married to his once fulltime nurse
A practicing lawyer, published writer

A tragic loss
Reality hits home
Loss of my own blood
The untimely death of a functioning, loving being

Like a wolf in the night
The virus steals its prey
Families stunned, loved ones grieve
Another number added to the curve
Sadly, I know the person behind the number
The throat burns, the gut churns

Good Friday

Good Friday
Crucifixion
COVID-19
Scourge of population

Pandemic
World trauma
Tears and sorrow
Pain's aura

Sorrowful Mother
Bent in agony
Family of the victim
Confused, grief-laden

What is good about Good Friday?
Resurrection is coming
Healing
Joining

Darkness to light
Fear to connection
Outcome assured
Not to human expectation

Mystery unfolds
The alchemy of gold

Not Knowing

To know—the natural human desire
To not know—the natural spiritual mystery
In the chaos of global crisis
In the shuttered businesses of the world
In the fear and recklessness that abound
Listen from within
Let go of reaction
Try prudence, social responsibility
Find peace in not knowing
Let mystery unfold
Be guided by soul

Final Surrender

No need to change anything
Embrace everything
Discover you are one with all
Nowhere to go, nothing to acquire
Let go of resistance
Awaken to Truth
Love is the answer
Let everything belong
Seek the reality that transcends time
Let go of fear
The final surrender

Forecast Unknown

Springtime weather
Birds sing, fish jump
Coronavirus infects an at-risk nation
Corruption rampant, a country divided
Contempt sickens democracy
The virus finds a vulnerable prey
President feuds
Loved ones grieve their dead
COVID mothers separated from their newborns
Civic unrest rampant
Trump is trumped
Some curves flatten, others spike
Protesters rally
Spring blooms, people Zoom

Tomorrow's prediction cloudy and scary
The country in a horrific storm
Population in different boats
Yachts and dinghies
Some sadly drifting over the once imagined abyss of
the unknown, some pushed
See the name on vessels carrying the groups
Rich, Poor, Equality for All, Over 65, Exhausted,
Essentials, Non-Essentials, Millennials, Need Work,
Work from Home, Let Me Out, Out of Money,
Oppressed, Schooled from Home, At Risk, Wanna See
My Grandkids, Just Want to Feel Good Again and
more

The perennial hope
The sun will shine soon

Thesaurus on COVID

Fear, stunned, confused
Shocked, baffled, bemused
Bored, hopeful, mad
Poor, rich, sad
Overwhelmed, deadly, lazy
Sick and tired, fake news, crazy
Out of steam, compliant, rebellious
Rattled, aghast, industrious
Bewildered, yearning, dazed
At peace, puzzled, fazed

Now, try to find *your* nuclear word
It would be like an attempt to split the COVID atom
or
Listen to nightly newscasts
To hear the echo of the explosion

Mantra

New mantra for the nation
"Together While Apart"

Lester Holt's *Nightly News* sign off on NBC
"Please take care of yourself and each other"
~the better mantra for me

Center of Your Being

Remove the noise
   what is left?
Remove the clutter
   what do you see?
Remove the chaos
   how do you feel?
Remove the grudges
   what happens to the heart?
Remove hate
   what is the replacement?

Find the soundless core
      the empty space
      the place of rest

Choose the center of forgiveness
         the center of love
         the center of your being

Lockdown or Liberty

Lock down
Shutter arenas, shops, eateries
Keep distant, wear masks, shelter in place
Work from home, lose your livelihood
or
Open up
Go back to work, school, familiarity
Bring on the athletes, the entertainers
Sit in Starbucks, eat at Chili's

Listen to these—

Patrick Henry, American orator and founding father:
"Give me liberty or give me death."
Could liberty too soon cause more death?

Sir Thomas More, saint and English counselor:
"If the lion knew his own strength, hard were it for any man to rule him."
If a pandemic is a lion, can we rule it?

Anthony Fauci, American physician and immunologist:
"Sooner or later, you're going to see a surge of cases."
Facts do not lie. Prudence is wise. Watch.

Can we be kind?
Can we embrace both/and, with openness, strength and prudence?

A Lounge Chair's Lament

You seem to sit in me all the time
Now that you are here more than gone
I know you've loved me since the first day home
But heck, I'm your lounge chair, not your mom

When you used to leave the house
It was game-on behind your back
I would swivel, rock and spin
To imagined Zumba, in fact

I love my time alone
I'm not sat on or reclined in
So peaceful for me then
Until you show up again

I like space for me
I don't get in anymore
I'll be glad when quarantine lifts
So I can see you to the door

Psalm for a Pandemic

Oh, Lord
Your earth cries out to you
With tears of lament
Grief consumes the planet
To you we ask reprieve
You are the Great One
You are the Healer
May we put our trust in you
Remove our blinders where we have injured
  ourselves, others, our home planet
Show us compassion as we show compassion for
  the sick and dying, oppressed and abused
Give us a sign all shall be well
Save us from this time of travail
Let hope be in our hearts

Silver Lining

Silver lining
where bright light outlines clouds of dusk
    even when the world quakes in pandemic
    even when so many grieve, suffer
where love conquers fear
    even when nurture falls short
    even when luminosity grows dim
where peace surpasses all understanding
    even in disturbance
    even in mystery
Can you find a silver lining?

Big Words, Big Numbers, Big Names

Immunology, psychology
Pandemic, endemic
AIDS/HIV
COVID-19, Plague of Antonine
Yellow Fever, Black Death
Bubonic Plague, Plague of Justinian
Cholera, Influenza
Measles, Smallpox
How many lost?
Hundreds of millions lives snuffed over the millennia

Big words, big numbers, big names

Bill Gates: The greatest threat to humanity is
infectious disease.
Donald Trump: It will just go away and I'm doing a
wonderful job.

How do you see the big picture?
What have pandemics cost you?
How do you need to be educated?
What are you called to do?

Pandemic

Let the wisdom of uncertainty guide us
To hold the tension of opposites
To remember souls are eternal
To embrace the oneness of all

Weaned from the breast of dependency
May people find new paths

How shall we reach out to others?
How shall we receive help?
How shall we use money?
How shall we spend time?
How shall we practice self-care?
How shall we do our part?

In a global event of pain and suffering
Can compassion bring nations together?
Can peace be cultivated rather than war?
Can kindness be the new normal?

Bless What We Can

Seasons change
Fevers spike
Pathogens thrive
Some people breathe deeply
Many cannot

Who is next? When will this end?

A president blames everyone but himself
Pandemic ravages poor and rich
Police brutality rampant on video

Common people become kingpins
they risk, they care, they voice
they grieve, they sing, they help

Reach out, practice compassion in hope for a better
future
Bless what we can
While the seasons march to the beat of a different
drum

Gentle Boldness

Needs—a human condition, a universal reality
Basic needs like food and shelter
Plus necessary needs as being heard, belonging, validation
Having needs is needy
Often seen as weakness, treated with shame and rules

An important question, can neediness be sacred, holy?
Can needs be honored gently, boldly?
What if instead of judging needs, we hold human neediness with compassion
Like we would hold a small child and whisper, "It's okay. I see you. I hear you."
Gently, boldly

Allow gentle boldness to embrace us
Let the essentials of human existence be nurtured
Gently, boldly aware

It is time to be life-giving
Time to say yes to needs
With kindness, even in disruption
Let gentle boldness lead the way

Choices

The ache of no hugs for a grandchild
   or shall I hug anyway?

The conflict of losing one's livelihood
   or shall I show up for work?

The call to demonstrate in a pandemic
   or shall I take another course?

The separation from the dying or a newborn
   or shall I chance contamination?

The pain of choosing between good and good
   or shall I choose a gamble?

The dilemma of yes or no
   or shall I avoid responding?

The question of is prudence the best solution
   or shall I take a risk?

The push and pull of decision-making
   like being powerless to change the flow of flood
   waters, hoping to stay out of harm's way
In the rush of COVID
   may we choose wisely

Drink In

Drink in patience and humble ease
Qualities of being
Like with a child, be gentle
Playful, curious, inspiring

Drink in yearned-for qualities
Quench the longing heart
Like watering small seedlings
So they are supported from the start

Drink in sweet, warm virtue
Soothing as herbal tea
Bathed in hope and peace
Sip intentionally

Drink in what you thirst for
Lovingkindness at its best
Qualities of compassion
Let its sweetness be the test

Invitation

Write *your* own thoughts or poem here, then pass it on.

Peace be
with You